Beginning the Journey

Contents

Introduction—The Seasons of Marriage

Beginning the Journey

Into the High Country 11
Companionship and Friendship 17
Encourage Your Uniqueness 25
The Expression of Love 31
A Word to Husbands 39
A Wife's Expression 43
Forgiveness and Healing in Marriage 45
Guidelines for Marriage 53
A Prayer for Lovers 55

Becoming Parents

What Is a Family 59
Communication Guidelines for the Family 63
A Child—God's Reflection 69
The Calling of a Father 75

The Parenting Years

The Purpose and Calling of Parenthood 79
Guidelines for Parents 85
Home Is a Shelter 93
A Model for Our Love 97

Contents
(continued)

Our Mid-Life Years

The Potential of Mid-Life 103
Change 105
Adequacy 109
Launching Your Children 111
The Expanded Family 115
Guidelines of Wisdom and Instruction 119

Looking to the Future

Growing Older 123
Our Attitude Toward Life 125
The Resources We Need to Move Through Life .. 129
Our Exit and Entrance 135
Our Heavenly Family 139
Our Final Stage of Life 141

Introduction

The Seasons of Marriage

The imagery of seasons describes the journey of one's life as well as a couple's journey through their marriage. Our life alone or together is a journey which follows a basic sequence and progression—not always smooth and orderly.

Individual and family life cycles carry two important features. As an example, a cycle carries the idea of a process or journey from birth to conclusion (death). Then within this life cycle are stages or periods which here are called seasons.

Daniel Levinson talked about the meaning of seasons:

> There are qualitatively different seasons, each having its own distinctive character. Every season is different from those that precede and follow it, though it also has much in common with them. The imagery of seasons takes many forms. There are seasons in the year: spring is a time of blossoming, winter a time of death but also of rebirth and the start of a new cycle. There are seasons, too, within a single day—daybreak, noon, dusk, the quiet dark of night.[1]

The seasons of a marriage cannot be separated from the seasons of an individual's life or development.

The marital journey has been well described by Dr. Mark Lee:

Anyone who has ridden in an old New York subway car will recall his sensation of pitching and rolling as the train raced along worn tracks or slowed to a stop in a station. Standing passengers move as one body back and forth with the car's sway and changing velocity. All that prevents a pile-up of bodies on a turn or quick stop are the overhead straps. Almost oblivious to what is happening, passengers grip a strap, automatically tightening and loosening their holds to meet changing situations. In their free hands they hold books, or newspapers which they avidly read.

The experience may be made an analogy to marriages. A marriage changes pace, speeds along, even stops. Tracking is sometimes smooth, sometimes irregular. Tunnels and open spaces alternate. Those who take the ride sometimes relax, and sometimes hold on for dear life.[2]

A lobster is protected by an extremely hard shell. But he develops by growing and shedding a number of these hard shells. He must shed his shell. This is necessary but leaves him exposed and vulnerable. Eventually a new shell develops. This then is what occurs as we travel the journey of marriage.

[1] *The Seasons of a Man's Life,* Daniel Levinson, Ballantine Books, N.Y., 1978, p. 67.

[2] *Time Bombs in Marriage,* Mark Lee, Christian Herald Assoc., Chappaqua, N.Y., 1981, p. 91.

CELEBRATION OF MARRIAGE

—1—

Into the High Country

Before beginning any journey, you must select a path. One path out of many possible paths. And you don't always know the terrain that you will cover until you start.

Unlike the average high-country hiker, a person starting out on the marriage path can't pore over a Forest Service map or interrogate a ranger about the trail ahead. Neither does he have the advantage of trailside signs telling him in advance the exact distance, or whether the trail is classified as easy, moderate or difficult.

Picture a hiker standing at the base of a mountain. He must select a path. Not one of the paths is completely level; not one of them is an easy, downhill glide. Each of them will involve work, energy, patience, endurance and a steady pace.

As he steps onto a trail and begins the gradual ascent, the hiker has time to note and delight in his surroundings. He is fresh and rested. He sets a moderate pace. Having made adequate physical preparation, he does not feel winded or weary. He takes in the sounds of wildlife and the wind in the trees. His sense of smell awakens to the aroma of forest and flower. His eyes cradle scenes of vivid paintbrush and columbine, aspen bark and budding pine cone, the stationary chipmunks on rocks and stumps and the ever-alert hawk gliding silently overhead.

By stopping occasionally, the hiker is able to fully enjoy the experience and not exhaust himself; he conserves his energy and renews his strength.

Think of your marriage as a journey similar to that of the hiker.

Has it been like the experience just described? Or has it seemed like such a frantic race to get somewhere that you've missed too much along the way?

Have you paused now and then to get your bearings, check your directions and renew your strength?

Have you sufficiently planned for your marriage, as the hiker planned for his journey, by evaluating and clarifying your expectations, determining what you were bringing to your marriage that would help it succeed?

Did you, as a hiker must, select goals for your marriage and determine when to reach those goals?

Where is your marriage going?

Where do you want it to go?

Too many marriages are characterized by endless activity which is devoid of satisfaction for either person and which fails to build the marital relationship.

As the hiker continues his wilderness trek, his trail steepens and curves. It takes greater attention and effort to proceed successfully. At times, rocks and boulders are part of the path. Occasionally one must detour in order to avoid an obstruction such as a fallen tree. The experienced and seasoned hiker learns to accept and deal with problems on the path in such a way that he loses none of the enjoyment of his surroundings. He does not concentrate upon difficulties of the trip to the extent that he ignores and bypasses the benefits of being where he is.

This is a lesson for the marital journey as well. As challenges, difficulties, conflicts and problems arise (and they will), too often they consume the entire attention and energy of the couple. Instead of focusing on the pleasures and enjoyment that are still present, the couple allows these to be overshadowed. Yet this positive side of marriage can render the other experiences more livable, and can be used to sustain and build the relationship.

From: *Into The High Country*, H. Norman Wright, Multnomah Press: Portland, Oregon, 1979, p. 8,9.

Jesus' first act of public ministry was performed in the service of a marriage. He was at a wedding feast where the wine had run out. There he brought out the best wine *for* people. And for the rest of his life, wherever he went, he brought out the best wine *in* people. John the evangelist concludes the Cana story with the remark that the incident was a sign that brought belief among Christ's friends: "He let his glory be seen, and his disciples believed in him" (John 2:11). But perhaps Christ's "glory" lay not so much in the "miraculous" as in the "unexpected." Consistently he chose to do the unexpected in relating to others and thus found himself at the center of the community. It was not a community of the curious. It was a community of the restored. It was not a group of people held together by the question: "What will he do next?" They were people who had been taken by surprise because of the unexpected way this man put them in touch with their own best possibilities.

Jesus' ministry reveals the unexpected way of relating partnership to community. It dismantles the tit-for-tat arrangement on which we base our relating to others: "You fill my needs, I'll fill yours." It means making of our partnership a sign where friends might believe that the unexpected is possible. It suggests that marriage is more than drinking someone else's wines for our own nourishment. It is a reminder that we are also called to the marriage feast to give others the chance to discover what they least expect: that their best wines have yet to be poured.

Reprinted from: *Partnership Marriage and the Committed Life,* Edward R. Dufresne, by the Missionary Society of St. Paul the Apostle in the state of New York, Paulist Press, New York, 1975, p. 72.

—2—

Companionship and Friendship

We were created for companionship: "And God said, 'It is not good for the man to be alone.' " Companionship is one of the reasons we were created male and female. Friendship is part of God's intention for marriage. If a friendship occurs before marriage, and if it matures during the marriage, a couple will have the stability and the relationship needed to weather the crises of change which will occur over the years. Louis Wyse describes marital friendship like this:

> Someone asked me
> to name the time
> our friendship stopped
> and love began.

Oh, my darling,
that's the secret.
Our friendship
Never stopped.

From: *Into The High Country*, H. Norman Wright, Multnomah Press, Portland, Oregon, 1979, p. 23.

The car pulled to a halt at the end of a narrow, bumpy road winding through a forest. Before us was a break in the trees through which we could see a wide expanse of Cottonwood Creek in the Grand Teton National Park. My friend and I got out of the car and soon had on our hip boots and fishing accessories. We started across the stream at the shallowest point we could find. I went much slower than I usually do, for this was my friend's first experience at wading through the rushing waters. We paused in the middle of a sand bar and without saying much we both enjoyed the beauty around us. Tall cottonwood and aspen trees abounded; through them we could see the snow-tipped peaks of the Teton range.

Before us lay another segment of the stream, through which the water rushed so deep and fast that wading was impossible. One at a time, we had to delicately walk over a 20-foot log that spanned the stream. Once across the log, I left my equipment, went back and carried my friend's equipment over. Then I waited as the other slowly and cautiously inched across the log. I gave silent and verbal encouragement and suggestions until the crossing was made. Then we went on, talking, wading through small pools and tributaries, fishing, laughing, and sharing.

Wild flowers were everwhere—paintbrush, columbine, balsamroot, blue harebells and lupine. From time to time we would call one another's attention to a new flower or new cluster that we stumbled upon. We waded through another section of the stream and into a marshland where the water deepened quickly. Since my companion was not as tall as I, the water came very close to the top of the waders, and walking was much more difficult. As we pushed and plunged through this grassy and watery section, my friend held onto my belt in order to follow in my footsteps and avoid a sudden dropoff. Breaking clear of this portion of the river, we were faced with water that was clear, but rushing rapidly. I kept on going and looking ahead until I heard a call to stop. My weight and height enabled me to walk through this portion of the stream, but the force of the water was almost too great for my friend. So we tried walking close together and timing our steps. When both of my feet were planted firmly upon the rocky stream bottom, my fishing partner took a step. When the other's footing was firm, I took a step. As we cooperated and worked together, we made progress. My friend was willing to try a new activity over unfamiliar terrain. I was willing to slow my pace to accommodate another's ability.

As we neared the other side of the stream and I started to climb on top of a log, I looked across at an island 30 feet away and came face to face with a mother moose. I stopped, touched my companion, and pointed silently. As we watched, a calf ambled to its feet and gave us the once-over. Then mother and calf went back to their leisurely pace of selecting the choicest portions of the leaves for breakfast. We carefully circled the island, keeping our eyes on the mother moose in particular, and continued our journey down the river. Soon we reached the point where the Cottonwood and Snake rivers joined.

A few hours later we reached our car, physically exhausted, thirsty, and hungry. But it had been a time of enjoyment, a time that we would remember. This fishing excursion was a bit different for me. I went more slowly than usual and traveled a shorter distance. I took more time to notice my surroundings instead of spending every moment concentrating upon catching cut-throat trout. It was a new experience for my friend, and I wanted that friend to enjoy what I had been enjoying for many years. This person is very special, for she is my wife.

From: *Into The High Country*, H. Norman Wright, Multnomah Press, Portland, Oregon, 1979, pp. 20-23.

I Need You

I need you in my times of strength
   and in my weakness;
I need you when you hurt
   as much as when I hurt.

There is no longer the choice
   as to what we will share.
We will either share all of life
   or be fractured persons.

I didn't marry you out of need
   or to *be* needed;
We were not driven by instincts
   or emptiness;
We made a choice to love.

But I think something supernatural
   happens at the point of marriage commitment
   (or maybe it's actually *natural*).
A husband comes into existence;
   a wife is born.
He is a whole man
   before and after,
but at a point in time
   he becomes a man who also
   is a husband;
That is—a man who
   needs his wife.
She is a whole woman
   before and after.
But from now on

she needs him.
She is herself
  but now also a part of a new unit.

Maybe this is what it means
  in saying,
     "What *God* hath joined together."
Could it be He really does something
  special at "I do"?
Something like His creation
  of a mother when
    a woman gives birth;
(something so real that
  neither can quite survive
    again without the other).
Joining together—in marriage—
  two self-sufficient beings
into an interdependence so real
That when you hurt I hurt
  (there's nothing I can do about it!).

Your despair is mine
  even if you don't tell
    me about it.
But when you do tell,
  the sharing is easier for me;
(To know *why* I hurt, no matter
  how frightening the cause,
    is easier than living
      with the theories
        that fear suggests).

And you also can then share
   from my strength in
      that weakness.

If we are one
   then perhaps you don't always
      carry the antibodies
         within yourself
            to fight every infection.
Some wounds are healed
   by resources carried
      in my part of the unit.

When part of a body is endangered
   all the rest gears to its
      defense.
Shouldn't that be true
   in a pair
      so committed
         they are called
            one flesh?

From: *Choosing to Love,* Jerry and Barbara Cook, Regal Books, Ventura, California, 1982, pp. 78-80.

—3—

Encourage Your Uniqueness

A marriage is composed of two unique creations of God. Both have received gifts that need nourishment in order to bloom. Wise partners hang on to each other with open hands so that neither suffocates in submission.

I must not only allow my wife to develop her interests and talents, I must encourage it. She then inspires me to explore my abilities and gives me the freedom even to fail. We don't grow in separate backyards, but side by side. We don't dream independently of each other, for we are one, yet two.

The home is not a place where one plant looms large and the other is dwarfed. The happy home finds two plants blooming with family fragrance, each rejoicing in the uniqueness of the other. Home also has plenty of room for some little plants, called children, to sprout and grow.

Love is giving room to grow.

From: *Forty Ways to Say I Love You,* James R. Bjorge, Augsburg Publishing House, Minneapolis, Minnesota, 1978, p. 20.

Probably one of the greatest things we can do for one spouse is to permit them "to be," to permit each other "to be," and to help each other to develop into the kind of person God has ordained each to become. This requires a good deal of listening, sensitivity, and awareness, rather than domination, or coercion to force the other into a mold or pattern. Just letting each "be" and encouraging each "to be" himself—this is respect. It is the kind of respect Christ had for people. Christ was sometimes disgusted and perhaps disappointed with people and especially with Peter. However, He did not try to force Peter to change, to make him over. Rather, He took Peter's good traits and He developed them and encouraged them and allowed Peter "to be" what he was destined to be (Matthew 17:1-17, 14:36ff., 27:58). Much the same kind of lesson comes from a study of the apostle Paul whose

destructive energy was channeled into constructive energy as he met Christ on the Damascus road (Acts 9:3,17,19; 22:6; 26:12). This concept is tremendously important in marriage because when we finally begin to accept each other, then we begin to mature.

From: *Everything You Need to Know to Stay Married and Like It*, Bernard R. Wiese and Urban G. Steinmetz, Zondervan Publishing House, Grand Rapids, Michigan, 1972, p. 139.

Let those of us who are already married with some degree of satisfaction give to our marriages the time, care, love, and energy that they deserve. If marriage—permanent, binding, faithful marriage—is so important to God's program that He chose it as a way of reflecting His eternal love for his people, then how high a priority should we give to it?

From: *Is the Family Here to Stay?*, David Allan Hubbard, Word Books, Waco, Texas, 1971, p. 27.

To Understand Each Other:

It is quite clear that between love and understanding there is a very close link. It is so close that we never know where the one ends and the other begins, nor which of the two is the cause or the effect. He who loves understands, and he who understands loves. One who feels understood feels loved, and one who feels loved feels sure of being understood.

From: *Equality and Submission in Marriage,* John C. Howell, Broadman Press, Nashville, Tennessee, 1979, p. 76.

Fortunate is the couple in whose relationship there is something which allows them both to experience grace —the accepting love which one does not need to earn, because it is present as a spontaneous expression of the relationship.

From: *Equality and Submission in Marriage,* John C. Howell, Broadman Press, Nashville, Tennessee, 1979, p. 104. Quoted in *The Intimate Marriage* by Howard J. and Charlotte H. Clinebell, p. 23.

—4—

The Expression of Love

. . . I am come that they might have life, and that they might have it more abundantly.

John 10:10

Romance is not made of shivers and tingles—in spite of what the movies may tell us! Romance is not even what we do—or don't do. Doing the right things may enhance romance, but basically romance is an attitude. It is a man and woman being alive to one another—not taking one another for granted. It is an atmosphere—a look that speaks more eloquently than words, a squeeze of the hand as you pass each other in a crowded room, a pat on the head or the shoulder for no particular reason. Romance is an element of fascination and delight that culminates in a deep desire to experience all of life with the one we love.

Romance helps make marriage the triumph it can be . . . a triumph that is both a gift from God, and one that "takes some doing."

—Colleen and Louis Evans, Jr.

From: *Together Each Day,* Joan Winmill Brown and Bill Brown, Fleming H. Revell Company, Old Tappan, New Jersey, 1980, p. 64.

And if you leave God's paths and go astray, you will hear a Voice behind you say, "No, this is the way; walk here."

Isaiah 30:21 LB

God is anxious to make His will known to you, but He rarely does so in a spectacular way. Usually, He quietly permeates your thoughts with His thoughts and patiently fills your spirit with His Spirit, so that naturally, and almost spontaneously, you just know that you know what His will is. In a Christian marriage God has two channels to work through. As the marriage expands and other members become Spirit-filled Christians too, God will seek to permeate the thinking and fill the spirit of all of you, so the decisions affecting all of you can be made without undue difficulty or dissension.

—John Allan Lavender

From: *Together Each Day,* Joan Winmill Brown and Bill Brown, Fleming H. Revell Company, Old Tappan, New Jersey, 1980, p. 77.

Let us love one another: for love is of God . . .

I John 4:7

I love you, not only for what you are, but for what I am when I am with you. I love you, not only for what you made of yourself, but for what you are making of me.

I love you for the part of me that you bring out.

I love you for putting your hand into my heaped-up heart, and passing over all the foolish, weak things that you can't help dimly seeing there, and for drawing out into the light all the beautiful belongings that no one else had looked quite far enough to find.

I love you because you are helping me to make of the lumber of my life not a tavern, but a temple; out of the works of my every day not a reproach, but a song.

You have done it without a touch, without a work, without a sign. You have done it by being yourself.

—Roy Croft

From: *Together Each Day,* Joan Winmill Brown and Bill Brown, Fleming H. Revell Company, Old Tappan, New Jersey, 1980, p. 43.

Two Lovers

Two lovers by a moss-grown spring:
They leaned soft cheeks together there,
Mingled the dark and sunny hair,
and heard the wooing thrushes sing.
      O budding time!
      O love's blest prime!

Two wedded from the portal stept;
The bells made happy carolings,
The air was soft as fanning wings,
White petals on the pathway slept.
      O pure-eyed bride!
      O tender pride!

Two faces o'er a cradle bent;
Two hands above the head were locked;
These pressed each other while they rocked;
Those watched a life that love had sent.

O solemn hour!
O hidden power!

Two parents by the evening fire;
The red light fell about their knees
On heads that rose by slow degrees
Like buds upon the lily spire.
O patient life!
O tender strife!

The two still sat together there,
The red light fell about their knees
But all the heads by slow degrees
Had gone and left the lonely pair.
O voyage fast!
O vanished past!

The red light shone upon the floor
And made the space between them wide;
They drew their chairs up side by side,
Their pale cheeks joined and said,
"Once more!"
O memories!
O past that is!

—George Eliot

Ideal Marriage: A Choosing to Love

I married a man I respect;
   I have no need to bow and defer.
I married a man I adore and admire;
   I don't need to be handed a list entitled
     "how to build his ego" or
     "the male need for admiration."
Love, worship, loyalty, trust—these are inside me;
   They motivate my actions.
   To reduce them to rules destroys my motivation.
I *choose* to serve him
   to enjoy him.
We *choose* to live together
   and grow together,
     to stretch our capacities for love
       even when it hurts
         and looks like conflict.
We *choose* to learn to know each other
   as real people,
     as two unique individuals
       unlike any other two.
Our marriage is a commitment to love;
   to belong to each other
     to know and understand
       to care
         to share ourselves
           our goals
             interests
               desires
                 needs

Out of that commitment the actions follow.
Love defines our behavior
    and our ways of living together.
And since we fail to meet not only the demands
    of standards but also the
        simple requirements of love
We are forced to believe in forgiveness
    . . . and grace.

From: *Choosing to Love,* Jerry and Barbara Cook, Regal Books, Ventura, California, 1982, pp. 18, 19.

    Marriages, then, (let's be more personal) our marriages, are supposed to be earthly, tangible, concrete, specific demonstrations of God's eternal covenant with His people. God does not quit. He sticks with His church through thick and thin, just as He clung to His people Israel in her crooked and perverse wanderings, as well as in her days of righteousness and justice.

    God's pledge never to leave us or forsake us is the prototype of our marriage vows. The greatest challenge we face in life is to let our lives in loyalty and love reflect God's constancy. Christ showed us the way by His own example: "Having loved His own who were in the world, He loved them to the end" (John 13:1).

From: *Is the Family Here to Stay?,* David Allan Hubbard, Word Books, Waco, Texas, 1971, p. 26.

—5—

A Word to Husbands

Headship is not at all a husband's becoming a master, boss, tyrant, authoritarion—the dominant, coercive force. Neither does it imply control or restriction, his being assertive and her being suppressed. It cannot mean he assumes any prerogatives of greater virtue, intelligence, or ability. It does not mean that he is active and she passive, he the voice and she the silent partner. Nor does it mean that he is the tribal chief, the family manager, the one who has superior rights or privileges. He is not the decision-maker, problem-solver, goal-setter, or director of everyone else in the family's life. Rather, he is, primarily for their common advance toward freedom and fellowship—

creating a partnership of equals under one responsible head.

From: *Marriage as Equal Partnership,* Dwight Hervey Small, Baker Book House, Grand Rapids, Michigan, 1980, p. 43.

Headship invests the husband with one more reason to be in subjection to Christ, his Head. Now he must function in a similar capacity toward his wife; he cannot do this on his own.

From: *Marriage as Equal Partnership,* Dwight Hervey Small, Baker Book House, Grand Rapids, Michigan, 1980, p. 42.

Paul says that a husband is to follow the loving model of Jesus. This means that to love one's wife means to provide opportunities for her to become sanctified, to grow in her experience as a human being toward her God-given potential. I see here the pastoral role of a husband, guaranteeing the spiritual experience of his family. The measurement of such a principle in our families is the answer to this questions:

Is your wife a more mature child of God because she is married to you?

From: *Magnificent Marriage,* Gordon MacDonald, Tyndale House Publishers, Inc., Wheaton, Illinois, 1976, p. 110.

Another principle of husband-love is that of presenting the church to the Father. One senses here the picture of Jesus Christ at the end of the age introducing the church formally to his Heavenly Father. Here is the church, Father, for which I have died, filled with my Spirit, and prayed for in my intercession ministry through the years. Our only conceivable image is a twofold one: the face of the proud groom at a wedding escorting his beautiful bride away from the marriage altar. But see the same man twenty-five years later, the marks of life etched upon his face and body. But his face is even more radiant as he stands for a 25th anniversary portrait surrounded by the family for which he has given so much.

So Christ stands before the Father and says in effect, the church is my most prized possession. I have given myself for it; I have cleansed it; and now it is worthy to be my bride, my highest achievement. I am blessed with the fact that the beauties of the universe are not enough to entice the eyes of the Savior. What he deems most attractive is the sanctified church.

From: *Magnificent Marriage,* Gordon MacDonald, Tyndale House Publishers, Inc., Wheaton, Illinois, 1976, p. 111.

—6—

A Wife's Expression

. . . but how can one be warm alone?
Ecclesiastes 4:11

I am married, I am married, and my heart is glad.

I will give thanks unto the Lord for the love and protection of my husband. I will give thanks for the blessed protection and satisfaction of my home. I will give thanks that I have someone of my own to help and comfort and even to worry about, someone to encourage and to love.

My husband is beside me wherever I need to go. My husband is behind me supporting me in whatever I need to do. I need not face the world alone. I need not face my family alone.

I need face only myself and God alone. And this is good. This is very good.

Whatever our differences, whatever our trials, I will give thanks unto the Lord for my husband and my marriage. For so long as I have both my husband and my God I am a woman complete, I am not alone.

—Marjorie Holmes

From: *Together Each Day,* Joan Winmill Brown and Bill Brown, Fleming H. Revell Company, Old Tappan, New Jersey, 1980, p. 127.

—7—

Forgiveness and Healing

Forgiveness is the cleansing agent which can clear the air of hostility in the home.

Forgiveness is needed when cruel and cutting words have been flung at mate or children or parents.

Forgiveness is needed when trust has been broken by the deliberate desire to deceive.

Forgiveness is needed when selfishness has caused us to ride roughshod over the rights of others in the home.

Forgiveness is needed when pregnancy is a reality for our unmarried daughter.

Forgiveness is needed when buried resentments toward parents are blocking our ability to love them in their aging years.

Forgiveness is needed when the spiritual cancer called hate is destroying our own peace with self and with God.

Forgiveness is the way to clean up the air pollution in our home life which can ultimately destroy our families, or separate us from each other so completely that we live in a vacuum of aloneness.

From: *Equality and Submission in Marriage,* John C. Howell, Broadman Press, Nashville, Tennessee, 1979, p. 101.

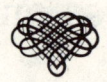

I can say to myself that the pain was so searing when you said that to me, or when you ignored me for such a long period of time, that I can't forget it. If I do I have decided to keep it lodged in my mind. If I remember the hurt rather than the reality of your asking forgiveness, then there's something wrong in me. The only way it can be healed is by my seeking forgiveness of you for considering an event or a situation to be more important than you. I can purposely recall the overwhelming presence of you at that moment when you said to me, "I really need you—not to excuse me, not just to straighten things out between us—but to forgive me."

With forgiveness there is healing and light hearts! Life is rich and joyous!

From: *Love Is a Couple,* by Fr. Chuck Gallagher, S.J., Worldwide Marriage Encounter, New York, New York, 1976.

God of all grace, teach us how to live on your terms. Help us as husbands to view our wives as honored, esteemed partners in your love. Help our wives to nurture their inward beauty. Show us the intimate connections between our spiritual lives and our marital responsibilities, and forgive us for fencing life into compartments. You have told us that effective prayer and faithful witness are dependent on how we treat each other. This scares us, but in our fear we want to seek fresh grace. We know your supply of grace never runs out because we have seen Jesus Christ who is full of grace. In His name we take courage to pray. Amen.

From: *Is the Family Here to Stay?,* David Allan Hubbard, Word Books, Waco, Texas, 1971, p. 36.

Forgiveness brings us closer together and cements our relationship. It makes us aware of each other's goodness. The person who has been forgiven is overwhelmed and awed by the mercifulness and the generosity of his beloved. The person who is extending forgiveness is thunderstruck by his partner's humility and love. Once we have forgiven each other, life will never again be the same between us.

Each time of forgiveness is a moment of maturing in a marriage. It is a coming of age and an advancement. It makes us both realize the potential we have in each other.

Forgiveness is a testimony to our experience of unity. Rather than just avoiding hurts in our relationship, or doing the right thing by each other, or living up to our responsibilities, we are reaching out for an integration of our two selves. We are intermingling our souls. Nothing has greater significance for a husband-and-wife relationship than our experience of forgiving and being forgiven by each other.

From: *Love Is a Couple*, by Fr. Chuck Gallagher, S.J., Worldwide Marriage Encounter, New York, New York, 1976, p. 141.

Healing between husband and wife is a beautiful experience. It is very real and magnificent. However, it is a catch-up situation. The reason healing is necessary is that the hurt has been devastating. We can't excuse our hurting each other on the basis that healing is meaningful; we have to try to reduce the hurts. The human dimension is such that, despite our best efforts and greatest concern, we will still hurt each other because of our selfishness or carelessness. We really don't want to, do we?

After all, our whole ambition in life when we first met and got married was to bring joy and happiness to each other. Hurt is contrary to that ambition. So if we're sincere in saying that we love each other, we definitely have to make a commitment to work together to reduce the hurts, both in frequency and in depth. And we can't do it unless we talk everything out. We have to find out what hurts the other person. All too often, even after years of marriage, we don't know what his hurt points are; we don't take them seriously enough; we don't realize how much certain words or actions sting. Caring, we'll find out. When we know, we can take steps to avoid the hurt.

From: *Love Is a Couple,* by Fr. Chuck Gallagher, S.J., Worldwide Marriage Encounter, New York, New York, 1976, p. 119.

We have to heal each other, come to grips with each other as persons, blend again, become one. This goes far beyond just deciding not to stay mad anymore, not to stay hurt, not to brood or withdraw. Healing calls for reconciliation. A couple needs to be aware of each other again; each has to be more aware of the other's hurt than his own. They have to want to remove that hurt, not just skip over it. Each has to make sure the other person is whole again.

From: *Love Is a Couple*, by Fr. Chuck Gallagher, S.J., Worldwide Marriage Encounter, New York, New York, 1976, p. 121.

In all probability the occasions of healing in our relationship are brilliant stars in our sky. It's good to reflect on them. Nothing is more refreshing, nothing can make me feel warmer toward you, than those moments when you put me together again, when you bring me back from the depths of hurt.

Healing has a tremendous immediate impact on us and we very much appreciate it, but sometimes we soon forget about it. When it passes again through my mind I may smile or feel very warm, but then go on to something else. Actually, the more I reflect upon the healing, continually making it alive to me, the more capable I will be of experiencing it again, and of granting that experience to you.

From: *Love Is a Couple*, by Fr. Chuck Gallagher, S.J., Worldwide Marriage Encounter, New York, New York, 1976, p. 120.

James 5:16—Admit your faults to one another and pray for each other so that you may be healed. The earnest prayer of a righteous man has great power and wonderful results. (LB)

Matthew 6:14,15—Your heavenly Father will forgive you if you forgive those who sin against you; but if you refuse to forgive them, He will not forgive you. (LB)

Colossians 3:13—Be gentle and ready to forgive; never hold grudges. Remember, the Lord forgave you, so you must forgive others. (LB)

Ephesians 4:32—Instead, be kind to each other, tenderhearted, forgiving one another, just as God has forgiven you because you belong to Christ. (LB)

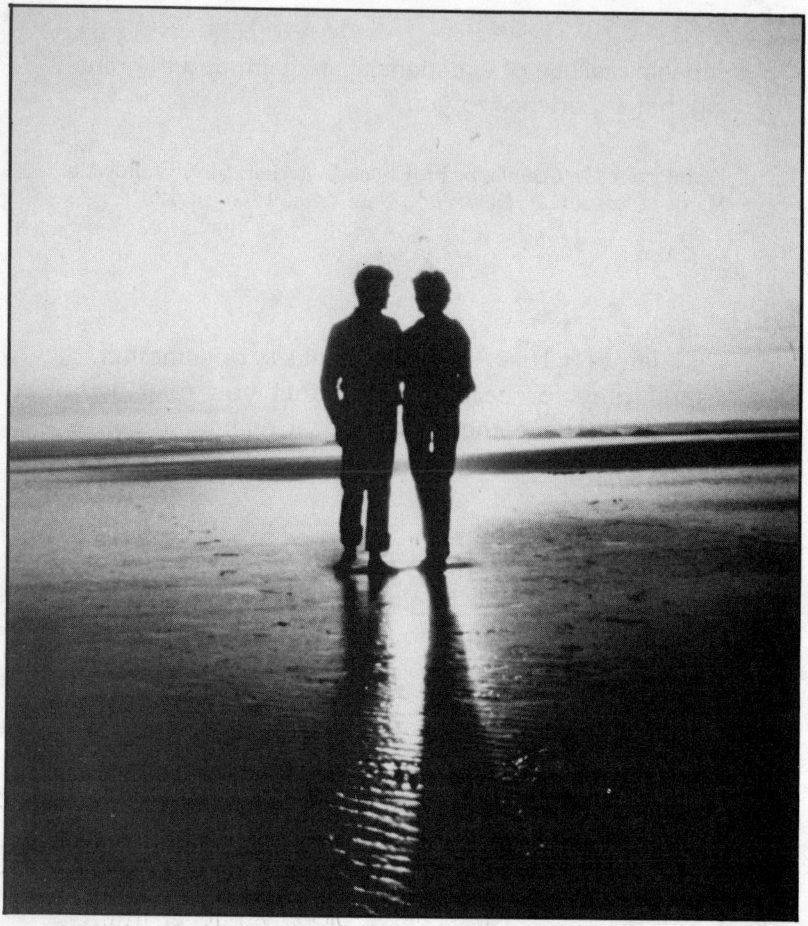

—8—

Guidelines for Marriage

I Corinthians 13:4-7—Love is very patient and kind, never jealous or envious, never boastful or proud, never haughty or selfish or rude. Love does not demand its own way. It is not irritable or touchy. It does not hold grudges and will hardly even notice when others do it wrong. It is never glad about injustice, but rejoices whenever truth wins out. If you love someone you will be loyal to him no matter what the cost. You will always believe in him, always expect the best of him, and always stand your ground in defending him. (LB)

Philippians 2:2-5—Fill up and complete my joy by living in harmony and being of the same mind and one in purpose, having the same love, being in full accord and of one harmonious mind and intention.

Do nothing from factional motives—through contentiousness, strife, selfishness, or for unworthy ends—or prompted by conceit and empty arrogance. Instead in the true spirit of humility (lowliness of mind) let each regard the other as better than and superior to himself—thinking more highly of one another than you do of yourselves.

Let each of you esteem and look upon and be concerned for not (merely) his own interests, but also each for the interests of others.

Let this same attitude and purpose and (humble) mind be in you which was in Christ Jesus—Let Him be your example in humility. (AMP)

Ephesians 4:2—Living as becomes you—with complete lowliness of mind (humility) and meekness (unselfishness, gentleness, mildness), with patience, bearing with one another and making allowances because you love one another. (AMP)

—9—

A Prayer for Lovers

Lord, we believe that You ordained marriage
  and that You also sustain it.
Help us to exercise faith.
  Faith that You answer prayer
    and heal wounded hearts.
  Faith that You forgive and restore.
  Faith that Your hand of love
    will clasp our hands together.
  Faith that You build bridges of reconciliation.
  Faith that all things will work for good
    to those who love You.

56/A Prayer for Lovers

Help us to hold on to hope.
    Hope that enables us to endure
        times of trial and testing.
    Hope that fixes our gaze on possibilities
        rather than problems.
    Hope that focuses on the road ahead
        instead of detours already passed.
    Hope that instills trust, even in the midst of failure.
    Hope that harbors happiness.
Help us to lift up love.
    Love that doesn't falter or faint
        in the winds of adversity.
    Love that is determined to grow and bear fruit.
    Love that is slow to anger and quick to praise.
    Love that looks for ways of saying
        "I care for you."
    Love that remains steady during shaky days.
    Lord, may Your gifts of faith, hope, and love find plenty of living room in our hearts. Thank you that these three abide—and the greatest is love. Make our home an outpost for Your kingdom and an oasis for wandering pilgrims. In the name of Jesus who blessed the marriage at Cana with a miracle. Amen.

From: *Forty Ways to Say I Love You,* James R. Bjorge, Augsburg Publishing House, Minneapolis, Minnesota, 1978, pp. 91-92.

Becoming Parents

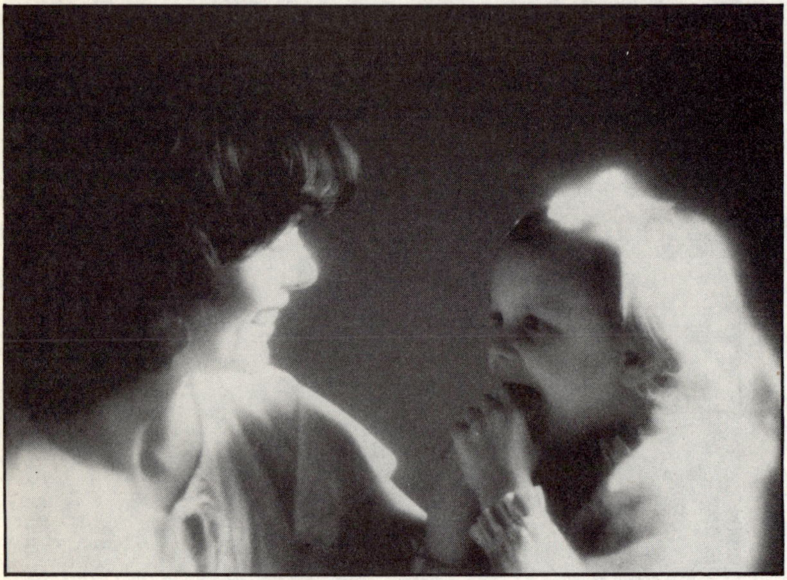

—10—
What Is a Family?

What is a family? A family is a mobile. A family is an art form. A family is an exciting art career, because an art form needs work.

God's mobile—a human being—two human beings—a family of human beings. Mobiles that can reproduce. Constantly changing patterns, affected by each other, inspired by each other, helped by each other. A family which is real in space and time and history, with roots in the past and stretching out into the future.

From: *What Is a Family?* Edith Schaeffer, Fleming H. Revell Company, Old Tappan, New Jersey, 1975, pp. 19, 24.

What is a family? A family is a blending of people for whom a career of making a shelter in the time of storm is worth a lifetime! A Christian family is meant to be different because of its knowledge that human beings are significant in this life and through eternity. A Christian family has been given enough in God's verbalized Word to know that when one part of the body hurts, the rest of the body is affected and does something to help. The rest of the body doesn't just "give up," but goes on. Because we have a handicap or broken ribs, a foot in a cast, dizziness or headache, we don't come to a DEAD STOP with the rest of our bodies—we go on in the best way we can.

From: *What Is a Family?* Edith Schaeffer, Fleming H. Revell Company, Old Tappan, New Jersey, 1975, p. 117.

Unity and diversity. Form and freedom. Togetherness and individuality. A family.

Age, youth, childhood, infancy—strung together on tiny threads. Blowing in delicate movement, independently, yet together. A family—belonging to each other, affected by each other, compassionate for each other, concerned about each other, interested in each other—a living mobile, never static. A family.

From: *What Is a Family?* Edith Schaeffer, Fleming H. Revell Company, Old Tappan, New Jersey, 1975, p. 30.

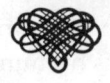

What is a family? A family is a well-regulated hospital, a nursing home, a shelter in time of physical need, a place where a sick person is greeted as a sick human being and not as a machine that has a loose bolt, or a mechanical doll that no longer works—to be shoved aside because it is no more fun, nor is it useful! A family should be a training place for growing human beings to know how to care for a great variety of sicknesses, and for people who have just had accidents or operations, because each one has received both knowledgeable and loving care, and has watched it being given to others.

From: *What Is a Family?* Edith Schaeffer, Fleming H. Revell Company, Old Tappan, New Jersey, 1975, p. 95.

The family is a gift of the Lord to mankind, a "room" in the creation for man's benefit. God did not leave man alone in an uncharted, unstructured world; rather, he so structured the world by his creative Word that man could know how to live. As a human community the family is structurally anchored in the law-order of God and takes its place as one of the central "rooms" in the creation.

Man comes to life in the family; he learns to love in the family. The family is his nursery, his first school; it is his initial world and his launching pad into the big outdoors. As he participates in the family, he experiences the diversity of life without having to bear full responsibility for all that happens. The family is his place of joy and sadness; it is the place where he learns to take and bear responsibility. In the family he learns to express his feelings and to know himself; he finds his identity; he experiences intimacy. Without the family the young child stands unprotected against the world. Without a family a child is alone, forced to live before he has even learned how. Nothing is more tragic than children worn out by life just when life should be opening up its riches.

From: *I Pledge You My Troth*, James H. Olthuis, Harper & Row Publishers, New York, New York, 1975, pp. 78-79.

–11–
Communications Guidelines for the Family

Ephesians 4:29—Let no foul or polluting language, nor evil word, nor unwholesome or worthless talk (ever) come out of your mouth; but only such (speech) as is good and beneficial to the spiritual progress of others, as is fitting to the need and the occasion, that it may be a blessing and give grace (God's favor) to those who hear it. (AMP)

James 3:5-10—Even so the tongue is a little member, and it can boast of great things. See how much wood or how great a forest a tiny spark can set ablaze! And the tongue (is) a fire. (The tongue is a) world of wickedness set among our members, contaminating and depraving the whole body and setting on fire the wheel of birth —the cycle of man's nature—being itself ignited by hell (Gehenna). For every kind of beast and bird, or reptile and sea animal, can be tamed and has been tamed by human genius (nature). But the human tongue can be tamed by no man. It is (an undisciplined, irreconcilable) restless evil, full of death-bringing poison. With it we bless the Lord and Father, and with it we curse men who were made in God's likeness! Out of the same mouth come forth blessing and cursing. These things, my brethren, ought not to be so. (AMP)

Proverbs 10:14—Wise men store up knowledge (in mind and heart), but the mouth of the foolish is a present destruction. (AMP)

Proverbs 25:15—By long forebearing and calmness of spirit a judge or ruler is persuaded, and soft speech breaks down the most bonelike resistance. (AMP)

Proverbs 25:11—A word fitly spoken and in due season is like apples of gold in a setting of silver. (AMP)

Proverbs 16:24—Pleasant words are as a honeycomb, sweet to the mind and healing to the body. (AMP)

Proverbs 15:23—A man has joy in making an apt answer, and a word spoken at the right moment, how good it is! (AMP)

Proverbs 15:4—A gentle tongue (with its healing power) is a tree of life, but willful contrariness in it breaks down the spirit. (AMP)

Proverbs 12:18—There are those who speak rashly like the piercing of a sword, but the tongue of the wise brings healing. (AMP)

Ecclesiastes 3:7—A time to rend, and a time to sew; a time to keep silence, and a time to speak; (Amos 5:13) (AMP)

Proverbs 10:19—In a multitude of words transgression is not lacking, but he who restrains his lips is prudent. (AMP)

Proverbs 15:31—The ear that listens to the reproof that leads to or gives life will remain among the wise. (AMP)

Proverbs 25:12—As an ear or nose ring of gold, or an ornament of fine gold, is a wise reprover to an ear that listens and obeys. (AMP)

Proverbs 23:12—Apply your mind to instruction and correction, and your ears to the words of knowledge. (AMP)

The family is God's first and foremost institution to fulfill His purpose in the world. From the creation of Eve, recorded in Genesis 1, through the last chapter of the Book of Revelation, Scripture uses the family to illustrate and demonstrate spiritual truth. Lockyer states:

> In the creation of home life on earth, with its love of husband and wife, parent and child, God designed to represent the love and blessedness of His home in heaven. At the heart of creation it was His purpose to people the earth with human

beings through whom the fulness of His love might flow out.

If God's purpose is to communicate His glory through creation, then the primary purpose of the family is to be a vehicle in this process. And if the family is to communicate God's glory, family members must be experiencing that glory. In other words, the family should be instrumental in promoting righteousness among its members because God is glorified when His character is reproduced in His children.

When we open Scripture, this is exactly what we find. The author of Hebrews states that the discipline of God and of our earthly fathers is designed to produce righteousness.

> Moreover, we have all had human fathers who disciplined us and we respected them for it. How much more should we submit to the Father of our spirits and live! Our fathers disciplined us for a little while as they thought best; but God disciplines us for our good, that we may share in His holiness. No discipline seems pleasant at the time, but painful. Later on, however, it produces a harvest of righteousness and peace for those who have been trained by it (Hebrews 12:9-11 NIV).

According to the Scriptures, parents and children live under the promises and demands of the kingdom of God. Family life must be integrated, deepened, and enriched by the leading of belief. "Honor your father and your mother, that your days may be long in the land which the Lord your God gives you" (Exodus 20:12). The family is part of God's covenant to His people. Within that covenant His faithfulness to His people is from generation to generation. Honor of father and mother is the law of the kingdom. Or as Paul puts it: "Children, obey your parents in everything, for this pleases the Lord" (Colossians 3:20 NIV). Why do children obey their parents? Because we are united in love in Christ. Our love for Christ shows up in the family room of the creation as honor, trust, and obedience to parents. Children must not forget this.

God desires the children to come to him by means of the parents. Thus, the Scriptures tell children to ask their parents about God and his mighty acts (Deuteronomy 32:7; cf. also Exodus 12; 26; 13:14; Deuteronomy 6:20; Joshua 4:6). In Deuteronomy God addresses the people. "And these words which I command you this day shall be upon your heart; and you shall teach them diligently unto your children, and shall talk of them when you sit in your house, and when you walk by the way, and when you lie down, and when you rise" (Deuteronomy 6:6-7).

Parents are God's representatives in their families. It is up to them to bring the Word in the family, and in turn to speak trustworthy words, and to do true deeds. They are to live this way because children naturally look to their parents for guidance.

From: *I Pledge You My Troth*, James H. Olthuis, Harper & Row Publishers, New York, New York, 1975, p. 93.

–12–

A Child—God's Reflection

When God wants a great work done in the world or a great wrong righted, he goes about it in a very unusual way. He doesn't stir up his earthquakes or send for his thunderbolts.

Instead he has a helpless baby born, perhaps in a simple home and of some obscure mother. And then God puts his idea into the mother's heart and she puts it into the baby's mind.

And then God waits.

The greatest forces in the world are not the earthquakes and the thunderbolts. The greatest forces in the world are babies.

—E. T. Sullivan

From the time of his conception, a Hebrew child was rightly regarded as one of God's most wonderful creations. No one knew exactly how the tiny embryo grew. One writer declared, "As thou knowest not . . . how the bones do grow in the womb of her that is with child: even so thou knowest not the works of God who maketh all. . .(Ecclesiastes 11:5)

The marvelous development of the child in his mother's womb seemed to be an extraordinary manifestation of God's goodness, for which the Psalmist offered his praise: 'Thou hast covered me (knit me together) in my mother's womb I will praise thee; for I am fearfully and wonderfully made (Psalm 139:13-14).

From: *Preparing for Parenthood,* H. Norman Wright and Marvin N. Inmon, Regal Books, Ventura, California, 1980, p. 152.

I love these little people; and it is not a slight thing when they, who are so fresh from God, love us.
—Charles Dickens

You can be very sure that the evil man will not go unpunished forever. And you can also be very sure that God will rescue the children of the godly. (Proverbs 11:21) (LB)

Reverence for God gives a man deep strength; his children have a place of refuge and security. (Proverbs 14:26) (LB)

Since the Lord is directing our steps, why try to understand everything that happens along the way. (Proverbs 20:24) (LB)

Teach a child to choose the right path, and when he is older he will remain upon it. (Proverbs 22:6) (LB)

He will keep in perfect peace all those who trust in Him, whose thoughts turn often to the Lord! Trust in the Lord God always, for in the Lord Jehovah is your everlasting strength. (Isaiah 26:3-4) (LB)

As for me, this is my promise to them, says the Lord: "My Holy Spirit shall not leave them, and they shall want the good and hate the wrong—they and their children and their children's children forever" (Isaiah 59:21) (LB)

———

Thus saith the Lord; Refrain thy voice from weeping, and thine eyes from tears: for thy work shall be rewarded, saith the Lord; and they shall come again from the land of the enemy. (Jeremiah 31:16)

———

Call unto me and I will answer thee and show thee great and mighty things which thou knowest not. (Jeremiah 33:3)

———

Therefore I will look unto the Lord; I will wait for the God of my salvation: my God will hear me. (Micah 7:7)

———

For Christ promised Him (The Holy Spirit) to each one of you who has been called by the Lord our God, and to your children and even to those in distant lands. (Acts 2:39) (LB)

They replied, "Believe in the Lord Jesus, and you will be saved—you and your household." (Acts 16:31) (NIV)

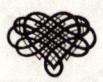

Scripture testifies that God created the universe to manifest His glory and His character.

And He intended mankind to participate in that glory and to be a reflector of it.

> It was His will that man on earth was to have points of resemblance to his Creator, and to prove in all his character and conduct that he was indeed created in God's image. In the domination he was to have over the earth, man was to exhibit the sovereignty and power of God as the King and Ruler of the universe.

From: *Parenting with Love and Limits,* Bruce Narramore, Zondervan Pub., Grand Rapids, Michigan, 1979, pp. 24, 25.

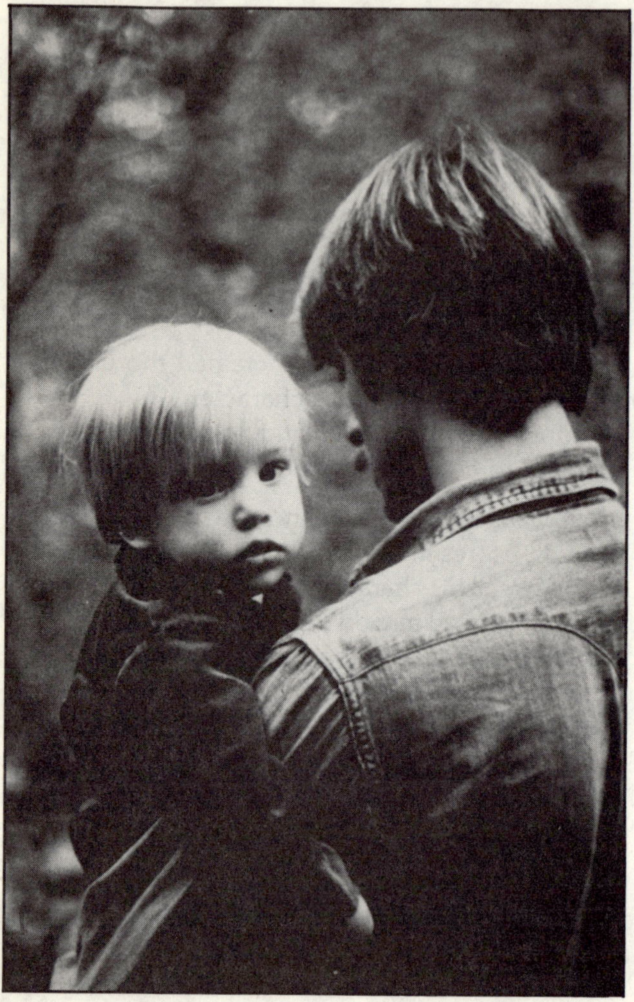

—13—

The Calling of a Father

"The effective father recognizes that fatherhood is a mandate from God, and he accepts the responsibilities and privileges it brings. He makes a major investment of his time and energy in this calling. He knows there will be enjoyable and difficult times, but he knows also that the God who called him to this unique ministry will sustain him through it.

"In his book *The Effective Father,* Gordon MacDonald uses the analogy of an orchestra conductor to describe the father's pacesetting role. In the analogy, the father is the conductor, his family is the orchestra, and God is the composer of the music. The father's task is to make sure the 'orchestra' plays the music the way the 'composer' wrote it. In other words, his job is to make sure the members of his family are living the way God intends for them to live.

"How does the effective father set this kind of pace?

—By expecting obedience from his children and following through to make sure he gets it.

—By protecting his children from harmful influences and supervising their character development.

—By developing good habits in his children's lives.

—By dealing directly with sinful or immature behavior.

—By teaching God's standards for living, as found in the Bible. (Deuteronomy 11:18-19.)

—By living before his children the kind of life he wants them to live. (Joshua 24:14-15.)

"All this develops a pace of life that his children can learn to follow."

From: *Preparing for Parenthood*, H. Norman Wright and Marvin N. Inmon, Regal Books, Ventura, California, 1980, p. 80.

The Parenting Years

—14—

The Purpose and Calling of Parenthood

The primary goal of child rearing, therefore, is to produce godly character in children so that God will be glorified. This perspective transforms the task of child rearing. Our goal is no longer merely to resolve family conflicts and find a little peace. Now we are participating in God's great program of the ages. We are shaping lives for eternity. We are helping to form each child's character so that he or she reflects God's glory.

From: *Parenting with Love and Limits*, Bruce Narramore, Zondervan Publisher, Grand Rapids, Michigan, 1979, pp. 25, 26.

John White, in *Parents in Pain,* says this about the parent in God's image:

Let me restate the basic rule of parenting: As God is to me so must I be to my children. As He has dealt with me, so must I deal with them. Such kindness as He has shown me, such patience and forebearing, such intolerance of sin—these must I in turn show to those for whom I stand in place of God. For in my children's minds a concept of God is growing which is derived from my spouse and me, two powerful beings who gave them birth and who seem to rule over the cosmos of the home. Each time my children see a godlike attitude or action in their father or mother, the Holy Spirit will tell them, "Now you can understand a little better what your Father in heaven is like."

Yet our striving to this higher goal must not be merely for our children's sake. Just as we are called to be holy because God is holy, so we are called to be parents because He is a parent, and that is reason enough. We were created in His image and to that image, even the image of God the Parent, we are called to be faithful.

One of the highest callings of Christian parents, then, is to build loving, sensitive, and honest relationships with their children, so that later in life these children can freely turn to God the Father, and readily accept His loving forgiveness.

What an incentive this is for parents to grow! Although our problems and sins may interfere with our child's relationship with God, our consistent love lays a foundation for meaningful faith in God.

From: *Preparing for Parenthood,* H. Norman Wright and Marvin N. Inmon, Regal Books, Ventura, California, 1980, p. 167.

Ephesians 6:4 says we are to nurture our children: "And, fathers, do not provoke your children to anger; but bring them up in the discipline and instruction of the Lord." Proverbs 22:6 reminds us that we are to train our children: "Train up a child in the way he should go, even when he is old he will not depart from it." Each of these will help our children feel that we are providing protection.

The parents' role in providing protection for their child is of emotional support so the child can meet head on the challenges and insecurity that life holds for him. This protection does not mean protecting our child from the possibilities of failure. Our child needs to understand that failure is all right; he is still accepted even though he is capable of making mistakes.

From: *Preparing for Parenthood,* H. Norman Wright and Marvin N. Inmon, Regal Books, Ventura, California, 1980, p. 163.

What do children need? And how well can parents meet their needs? Children need acceptance. They need praise and appreciation. They need to learn they can trust their parents not to deceive them or to break promises. They need consistency and fairness. They need to feel that their fears, their desires, their feelings, their inexplicable impulses, their frustrations, and their inabilities are understood by their parents. They need to now exactly where the limits are, what is permitted and what is prohibited. They need to know that home is a safe place, a place of refuge, a place where they have no need to be afraid. They need warm approval when they do well, and firm correction when they do wrong. They need to learn a sense of proportion. They need to know that their parents are stronger than they are, able to weather the storms and dangers of the outer world and also able to stand up to their (children's) rages and unreasonable demands. They need to feel their parents like them and can take time to listen. They need perceptive responses to their growing need for independence.

From: *Parents in Pain*, John White, InterVarsity Press, Downers Grove, Illinois, 1979, p. 181.

Just as the shepherd guards his sheep, so also are parents to guard their children from physical dangers and emotional perils and from spiritual attack. In their role as protector, parents are to provide for their children: "Here for this third time I am ready to come to you, and I will not be a burden to you; for I do not seek what is yours, but you; for children are not responsible to save up for their parents, but parents for their children" (II Corinthians 12:14 NASV).

From: *Preparing for Parenthood*, H. Norman Wright and Marvin N. Inmon, Regal Books, Ventura, California, 1980, p. 162.

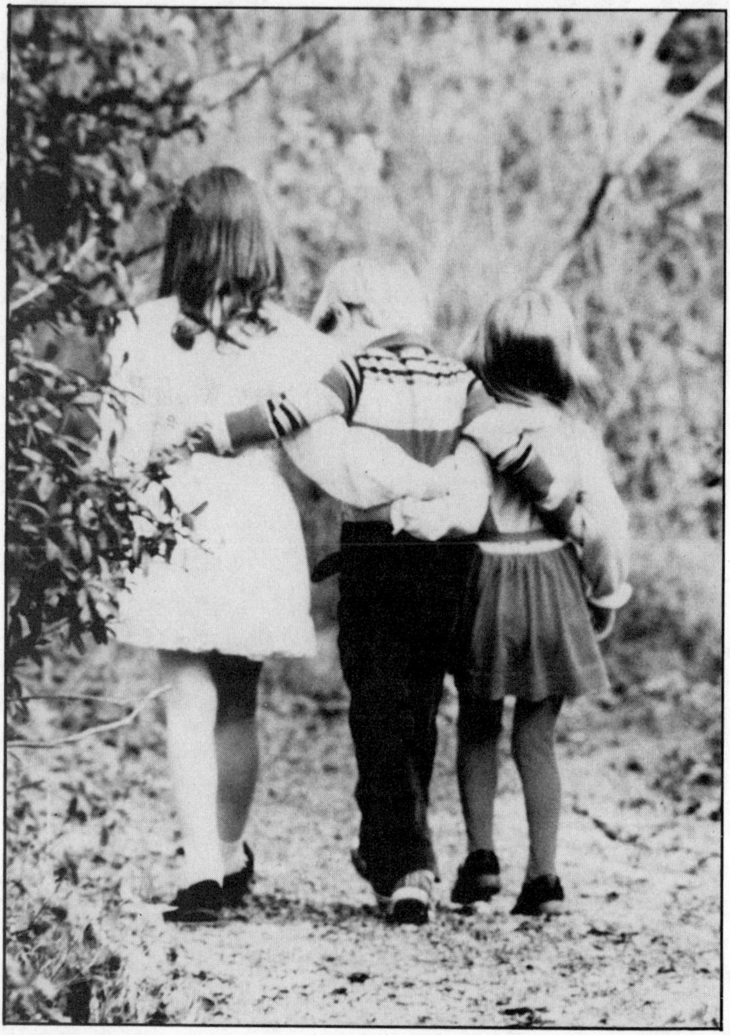

—15—

Guidelines for Parents

... But as for me and my house, we will serve the Lord. (Joshua 24:15) (KJV)

The Lord is close to the brokenhearted and saves those who are crushed in spirit. (Psalm 34:18) (NIV)

Trust in the Lord and do good; dwell in the land and enjoy safe pasture. Delight yourself in the Lord and He will give you the desires of your heart. (Psalm 37:3-4) (NIV)

Commit your way to the Lord; trust in him and he will do this: He will make your righteousness shine like the dawn, the justice of your cause like the noonday sun. (Psalm 37:5-6) (NIV)

Be still before the Lord and wait patiently for him; do not fret when men succeed in their ways, when they carry out their wicked schemes. Refrain from anger and turn from wrath; do not fret—it leads only to evil. (Psalm 37:7-8) (NIV)

Don't be impatient for the Lord to act! Keep traveling steadily along his pathway and in due season he will honor you with every blessing. . . . (Psalm 37:34) (LB)

For the Lord God is a sun and shield: the Lord gives grace and glory: no good thing does he withhold from those who walk uprightly. (Psalm 84:11) (NASV)

For the Lord is always good. He is always loving and kind, and his faithfulness goes on and on to each succeeding generation. (Psalm 100:5) (LB)

But the lovingkindness of the Lord is from everlasting to everlasting, to those who reverence him; his salvation is to children's children of those who are faithful to his covenant and remember to obey him! (Psalm 103:17) (LB)

Those who sow tears shall reap joy. Yes, they go out weeping, carrying seed for sowing, and return singing, carrying their sheaves. (Psalm 126:5-6) (LB)

Jehovah is kind and merciful, slow to get angry, full of love. He is good to everyone, and his compassion is intertwined with everything he does. (Psalm 145:8-9) (LB)

Trust in the Lord with all thine heart; and lean not unto thine own understanding. In all thy ways acknowledge him, and he shall direct thy paths. (Proverbs 3:5-6)

And we know that God causes all things to work together for good to those who love God, to those who are called according to His purpose. (Romans 8:28) (NASB)

From: *The Hurting Parent,* Margie M. Lewis and Gregg Lewis, Zondervan Publishing House, Grand Rapids, Michigan, 1980, Appendix, pp. 140-142.

Only be careful and watch yourselves closely so that you do not forget the things your eyes have seen or let them slip from your heart as long as you live. Teach them to your children and to their children after them. (Deuteronomy 4:9) (NIV)

Hear, O Israel: The Lord our God, the Lord is one. Love the Lord your God with all your heart and with all your soul and with all your strength. These commandments that I give you today are to be upon your hearts. Impress them on your children . . . . (Deuteronomy 6:4-7) (NIV)

Fix these words of mine in your hearts and minds; tie them as symbols on your hands and bind them on your foreheads. Teach them to your children, talking about them when you sit at home and when you walk along the road, when you lie down and when you get up. (Deuteronomy 11:18-19) (NIV)

When Moses finished reciting all these words to all Israel, he said to them, 'Take to heart all the words I have solemnly declared to you this day, so that you may command your children to obey carefully all the words of this law.' (Deuteronomy 32:45-46) (NIV)

He who spares the rod hates his son, but he who loves him is careful to discipline him. (Proverbs 13:24) (NIV)

Discipline your son, for in that there is hope; do not be a willing party to his death. (Proverbs 19:18) (NIV)

Train a child in the way he should go, and when he is old he will not turn from it. (Proverbs 22:6) (NIV)

Folly is bound up in the heart of a child, but the rod of discipline will drive it far from him. (Proverbs 22:15) (NIV)

Do not withhold discipline from a child; if you punish him with the rod, he will not die. Punish him with the rod, and save his soul from death. (Proverbs 23:13-14) (NIV)

Discipline your son, and he will give you peace; he will bring delight to your soul. (Proverbs 29:17) (NIV)

Fathers, do not exasperate your children; instead, bring them up in the training and instruction of the Lord. (Ephesians 6:4) (NIV)

Fathers, do not embitter your children, or they will become discouraged. (Colossians 3:21) (NIV)

Here is a trustworthy saying: If anyone sets his heart on being an overseer, he desires a noble task . . . He must manage his own family well and see that his children obey him with proper respect. (I Timothy 3:1,4) (NIV) If anyone does not provide for his relatives, and especially for his immediate family, he has denied the faith and is worse than an unbeliever. (I Timothy 5:8) (NIV)

From: *Parenting with Love and Limits,* Bruce Narramore, Zondervan Publishing House, Grand Rapids, Michigan, 1979, pp. 16, 17.

Proverbs 6:20—My son, keep your father's (God-given) commandment, and forsake not the law of (God) your mother (taught you). (AMP)

Proverbs 5:1,2—My son, be attentive to my wisdom (learned by actual and costly experience), and incline your ear to my understanding (of what is becoming and prudent for you); that you may exercise proper discrimination and discretion, and your lips guard and keep knowledge and the wise answer (to temptation). (AMP)

Proverbs 1:8—My son, hear the instruction of your father; reject not nor forsake the teaching of your mother. (AMP)

Proverbs 23:13—Withhold not discipline from the child, for if you strike and punish him with the (reed-like) rod, he will not die. (AMP)

Proverbs 22:6—Train up a child in the way he should go (and in keeping with his individual gift or bent), and when he is old he will not depart from it. (AMP)

Proverbs 19:18—Discipline your son while there is hope, but do not (indulge your angry resentments by undue chastisements and) set yourself to his ruin. (AMP)

Proverbs 13:24—He who spares his rod (of discipline) hates his son, but he who loves him diligently disciplines and punishes him early. (AMP)

Deuteronomy 6:4-7—O Israel, listen: Jehovah is our God, Jehovah alone. You must love him with all your heart, soul, and might. And you must think constantly about these commandments I am giving you today. You must teach them to your children and talk about them when you are at home or out for a walk; at bedtime and the first thing in the morning. (LB)

Psalm 127:3-5—Children are a gift from God; they are his reward. Children born to a young man are like sharp arrows to defend him. Happy is the man who has his quiver full of them. That man shall have the help he needs when arguing with his enemies. (LB)

—16—

Home Is a Shelter

By wisdom a house is built,
And by understanding it is established;
And by knowledge the rooms are filled
With all precious and pleasant riches.
Proverbs 24:3-4

The writer offers dependable counsel regarding the home. He is not referring to material things, such as matching drapes and carpet, a two-car garage, or a new sofa. No, these verses say the real answer does not rest in what we possess but in what we are. Your marriage will not be restored because you buy the right things but because you become the right one. These two verses don't even mention people. A home is built by wisdom . . . its structure is established by understanding . . . its rooms are enriched by knowledge.

From *Strike The Orginial Match,* Charles R. Swindoll, Multnomah Press, Portland, Oregon, 1980, p. 22.

Part of a family's function is to shoulder one end of our burdens and to share the delight of our blessings.

Robert Frost said, "Home is the place where, when you have to go there, they have to take you in." (The Death of the Hired Man). It is that, and a whole lot more. It is a center of fellowship, where families can be friends, where power and blessing abound.

Helping us to celebrate God's love is the chief blessing our families can give us. The unity that our psalmist calls "good and pleasant" is as much dependent on God as was the anointing oil that made Aaron a priest or the dew that watered Zion when there was no rain. Only as we know how much God loves each of us can we begin to know how to love each other.

Friendly families are not those where there are no differences or disagreements, but those where God's love provides the strong glue that binds them together whatever the differences may be. Families can be friends but only when true love takes charge. The Bible says this love comes from God. Have you found any better source?

From: *Is The Family Here To Stay*, David Allan Hubbard, Word Books, Waco, Texas, 1971, p. 79.

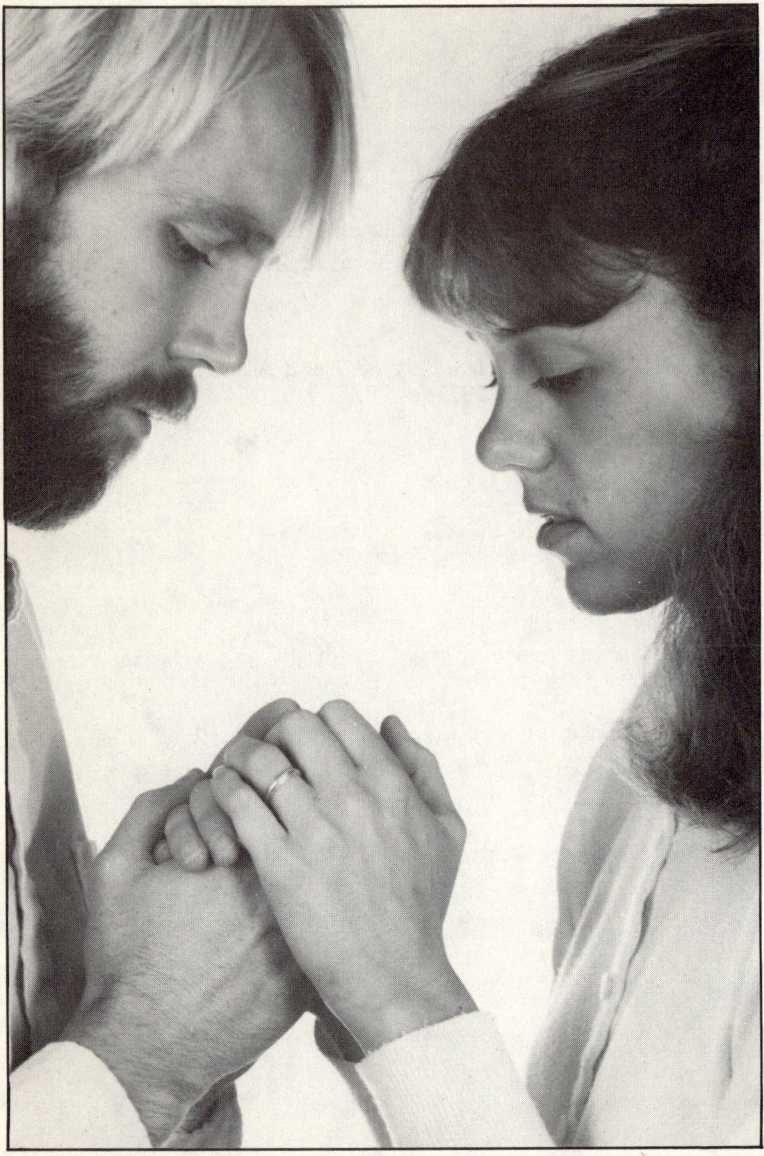

—17—
Model for Our Love

1. So patient and so kind. (Williams) It meekly and patiently bears ill treatment from others. It is gentle, benign, pervading and penetrating the whole nature, mellowing all which could have been harsh and austere. (Wuest)
2. This love looks for a way of being constructive. (Phillips)
3. It never boils with jealousy, never envies. (Williams and Amplified)
4. It is not conceited, arrogant, or inflated with pride. (Amplified)
5. It is neither anxious to impress nor does it cherish inflated ideas of its own importance. (Phillips)

6. It is not out for display. (Berkeley)
7. It does not act unbecomingly. (Wuest and Amplified)
8. It has good manners. (Phillips)
9. It covers up everything. (Berkeley)
10. It does not insist on its own rights or its own way —for it is not self-seeking. (Amplified)
11. It is not possessive. (Phillips)
12. It is not touchy, or fretful, or resentful. (Amplified)
13. It is not irritated, provoked, exasperated, aroused to anger. (Wuest)
14. It takes no account of the evil done to it. (Amplified)
15. It does not count up past wrongs. (Riverside, out of print)
16. It does not gloat over the wickedness of other people . . . It is glad with all good men when truth prevails. (Phillips)
17. Love knows no end to its trust. (Phillips)
18. It has unquenchable faith. (Berkeley)
19. It is ever ready to believe the best of every person. (Amplified)
20. It bears up under anything and everything that comes. Its hopes are fadeless under all circumstances, and it endures everything without weakening. (Amplified)

From: *Living Without Fear,* Wilma Burton, Good News Publishers, Westchester, Illinois, 1981, p. 120, 121.

Heavenly Father, we are frightened by our own fickleness. This makes your love all the more amazing. Give us the tenderness to be open to those who need our love. Let us learn to love from the one who wrote love's textbook, namely Jesus Christ. His love was so loyal and so lasting that He did not shirk even a cross for the sake of His bride. In His name and strength we pray. Amen.

From: *Is The Family Here To Stay?*, David Allan Hubbard, Word Books, Waco, Texas, 1971, p. 27.

Our Mid-Life Years

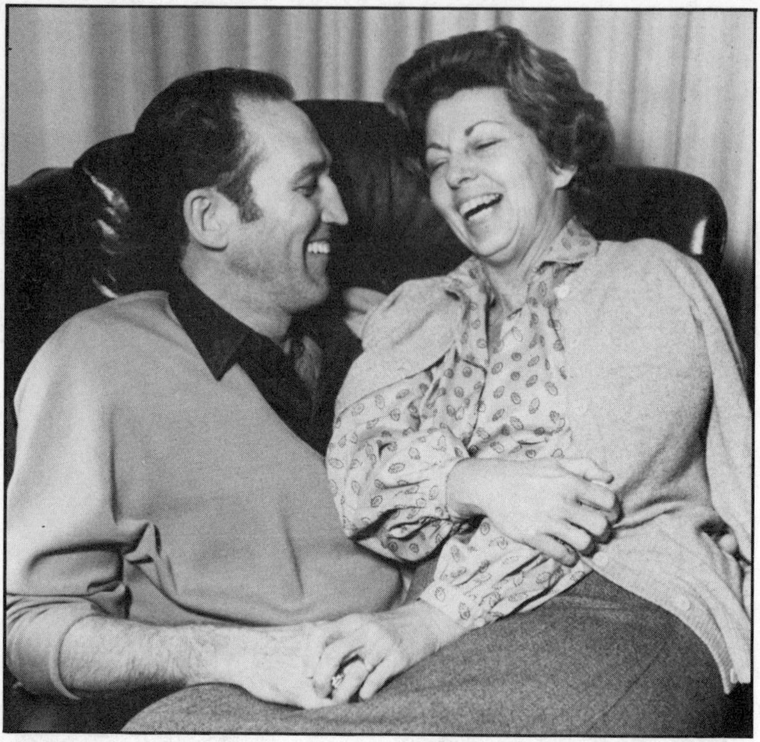

−18−

The Potential of Mid-Life

Middle-agers are beautiful!
    aren't we, Lord?
I feel for us
    too radical for our parents
    too reactionary for our kids
Supposedly in the prime of life
    like prime rib
        everybody eating off me
          devouring me
        nobody thanking me
          appreciating me
        but still hanging in there

> communicating with my parents
> in touch with my kids
> and getting more in touch
> with myself
> and that's all good
> Thanks for making it good
> and
> could you make it a little better?

From: *Lord, Could You Make It a Little Better?* Robert A. Raines, Word Books, Waco, Texas, 1972, p. 135.

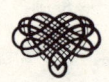

I believe that middle-aged marriage, lived as it should be and can be, offers qualities that nothing else has ever superseded: a shelter where two people can grow older without loneliness, the ease of long intimacy, family jokes that don't have to be explained, understanding without words. Most of all, it offers memories. The inexpressible sweetness of first love, a warm back in a wide bed, a child in a basket wearing its first smile, a sadder, shared surge of pride at a kid on a stage, a moment looking up at each other across a chessboard. Can these memories, having been shared, ever be replaced?

—Mackey Brown

From: *Growing Older,* Robert C. Leslie and Margaret G. Alter, Prentice-Hall, 1978, p. 96.

—19—

Change

It is the Christian who can deal most effectively with the impact of change in the stages of life. Firstly, the Christian believes that God has a specific plan for his life. He further believes that the plan He has for his life is one that God has already designed. It is also a plan that embodies not only the best for the person, but also for all of God's people. As Paul says in Romans 8:28, "All things work together for good to them that love God." This suggests that God has His hand in every turn of our lives. Therefore, what have we to fear? Now these are concepts to mouth, but to put them into working operation in our lives is something else again. It is hard at any moment of time to think that a disappointment or a tragedy can do anyone any good or can ever be part of a plan that God desires for that person's benefit. We, unfortunately—or fortunately—do not have eternal perspective. We see things from the point of view of a finite world. God, however, has the eternal blueprint. He can see beyond the brief events of our days.

It is by passing through the obstacles of middle life that we can gain the true maturity that Paul spoke of. In middle age, it is hoped the Christian is now quite familiar with God's Word. He has come to see it as the very blood of life that gives him sustenance for every day. He has seen experientially the power and efficacy of prayer. He has come to enjoy the incomparable fellowship of Christians. Each day the Person of Christ becomes more real to him. He sees in his own life a more perfect identification with the Person of Christ.

From: *Half-Way Up The Mountain,* David C. Moreley, M.D. Fleming H. Revell Co., Old Tappan, New Jersey, 1979 p. 49.

In order to make the most of this new crisis of self-discovery in middle age, one has, in a sense, to become a lobster—only knowing the danger, which I presume the lobster is happily free from experiencing! In order to fit into his shell as he grows bigger, the lobster goes through periodic sheddings of his shell. During these times he is naked and vulnerable and in terrible danger of being eaten by his enemies in the sea. And yet, in the inexorability of nature, he must go through this crisis of dangerous exposure, or not grow. So with middle age, it is possible to remain stationary, to accept life as one has lived it and to settle for more of what has been, good, bad, and indifferent.

From: *The Wonderful Crisis of Middle Age,* Eda J. LeShan, Warner Books, New York, New York, 1973, p. 21.

For a Christian, mid-life is a time when spiritual maturity can develop in its richest form, when the Person of Christ becomes a reality, the basis for a new and more meaningful relationship with Him, which allows us to include Him in every innuendo of our lives. It's the time of life when the Christian, in ways that seem paradoxical to the world, becomes stronger, because he is increasingly aware of the strength of his Lord. It is a time when the fruits of the Spirit begin to flourish with the ripeness that is even evident to those who are not Christian. It's a time when the Christian can feel a freedom from the superficial stimuli that entrap the minds of most men—the greed, the egocentricity, the lust, the self-deception, and the denial of many men lose their attractiveness.

Christians do not escape the cruel process of mid-life, but should be able to deal with this phase of their existence with greater sense of challenge than people who are not Christians. It is the peace, joy, and inner quietness that a Christian has available to him in the storms of mid-life that spark a more poignant message than the tongues of a thousand silver-tongued orators.

From: *Half-Way Up The Mountain,* David C. Morley, M.D. Fleming H. Revell Co., Old Tappan, New Jersey, 1979 p. 10, 11.

—20—
Adequacy

The writers of the Scriptures are careful to point out that when God looks at you in Jesus Christ, He sees you as a brother of His own Son. Because of the work of Christ, all the ugliness of humanity is set aside. God has absolutely no attitude of condemnation toward man. You are worth all of God's attention. If you were the only person in the world, it would be worth God's effort to make Himself known to you and to love you. He gives you freely the status and adequacy of an heir to the universe.

This is agape love, the unmerited, unconditional favor of God for man. We achieve our adequacy through this unceasing love. We do not become sufficient, approved, or adequate; rather we are declared to be such! When we believe this, we become achievers and humanitarians as an effect, a by-product of our newfound selves.

From: *Do I Have To Be Me?,* Lloyd H Ahlem, Regal Books, Ventura, California, 1974.

When a person has accepted adequacy as a gift, he immediately perceives a new standard for achievement. No longer does the criterion of human performance apply, but rather the measure of faithfulness judges us. This is the fair standard, the one that stimulates everyone, frustrates no one, and is administered by the providential will of God.

What is required of a man is that he be found faithful, to paraphrase I Corinthians 4:2. He should perform to the limits of his ability in the tasks God gives him to do. He should be free from social pressures to conform to the world's standards of achievement—free to do things he is truly able and motivated to do.

From: *Do I Have To Be Me?,* Lloyd H. Ahlem, Regal Books, Ventura, California, 1979.

—21—

Launching Your Children

Having children is a little like building ships. There comes a day when you have completed everything, and the ship needs to be launched. You christen it and send it sliding down to the sea of life. You trust it will not only float but sail. With your children, it's now up to God, and you trust Him even though you know all about the storms that may overtake them.

Taken from: *Change Points*, by Joyce Landorf, Fleming H. Revell Co., Old Tappan, New Jersey, 1981. p. 156.

To relinquish our children is to set them free. The earlier we relinquish them the better. If we unthinkingly view them as objects designed for our pleasure, we may destroy their capacity for freedom. We may also cripple ourselves. Having made our children necessary to our happiness, we can so depend on them that we grow incapable of managing without them.

From: *Parents in Pain,* John White, InterVarsity Press, Downers Grove, Illinois, 1979, p. 164.

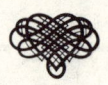

To understand what relinquishment is we must first understand what God is like and what the essence of His relationship to us is. As He is to us, so must we (so far as possible) be to our children.

God's attitude as a parent combines loving care and instruction with a refusal to force our obedience. He longs to bless us, yet He will not cram blessings down our throats. Our sins and rebellions cause Him grief, and in His grief He will do much to draw us back to Himself. Yet, if we persist in our wrongdoing He will let us find, by the pain of bitter experience, that it would have been better to obey Him.

To relinquish your children does not mean to abandon them, however, but to give them back to God, and in so doing to take your own hands off them. It means neither to neglect your responsibilities toward them, nor to relinquish the authority you need to fulfill those responsibilities. It means to release those controls that arise from needless fears, or from selfish ambitions.

From *Parents in Pain,* John White, InterVarsity Press, Downers Grove, Illinois, 1979, p. 165.

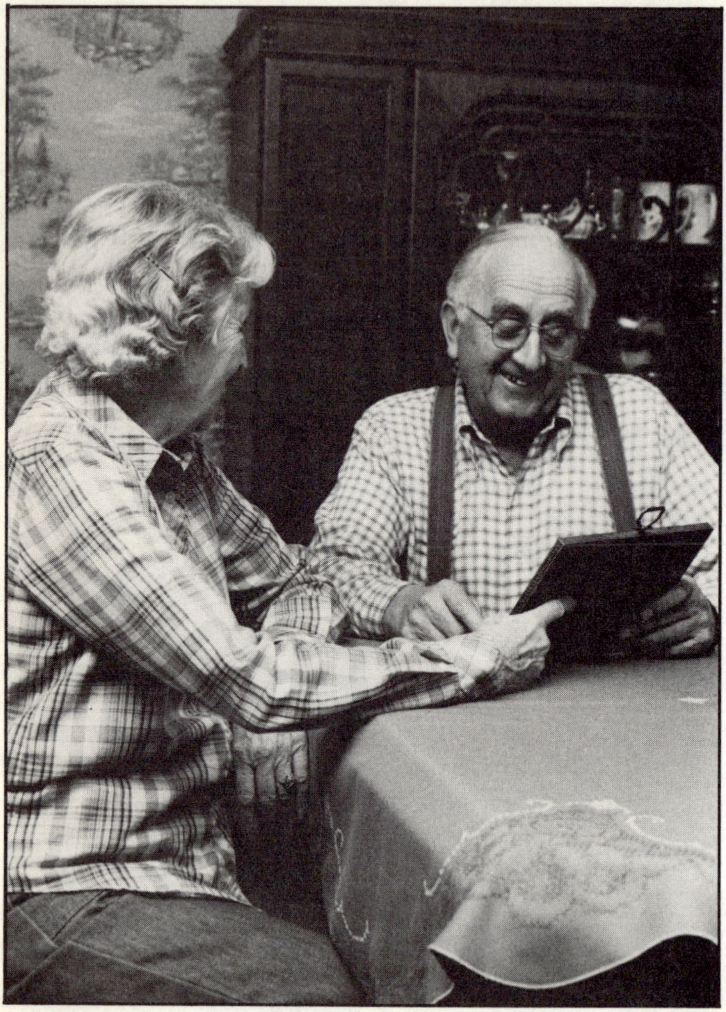

—22—

The Expanded Family

A family—parents and grandparents and children, the larger combination of three or four generations, or one little two-generation family—is meant to be a picture of what God is to His Family. "Hear my cry, O God; attend unto my prayer. From the end of the earth will I cry unto thee, when my heart is overwhelmed: lead me to the rock that is higher than I. For thou hast been a shelter for me, and a strong tower from the enemy" (Psalm 61:1-3). Our earthly family is meant to be a shelter, a solid, dependable "ear" that will hear and understand, as well as a place to which to run. Then this family, these parents, this father and mother, are to make clear to their children the understanding of the faithfulness of God. We should be able to say, "You know something of the way we love you. You can always come to us in any kind of trouble. You will always find forgiveness and understanding and help. Yet we are nothing in comparison to God, our Heavenly Father, whose faithfulness is perfect compared to our imperfection."

From: *What Is a Family?* Edith Schaeffer, Fleming H. Revell Company, Old Tappan, New Jersey, 1975, p. 51.

Family reunions, memories, little things to help keep the memories alive are not a luxury that takes too much time and effort and money, but a definite necessity on someone's part, if the mobile is to be beautiful and not lopsided and broken.

From: *What Is a Family?* Edith Schaeffer, Fleming H. Revell Company, Old Tappan, New Jersey, 1975, p. 26.

Family relationships are not just sentimental ideas; they are indispensable ties that keep us steady and secure amid the loneliness and uncertainty of life. Grandparents, aunts and uncles, parents, brothers and sisters play a very special part in our maturing. They show us something of where we have come from and what we will be. They are instruments of heredity and environment used by God to shape us for his purposes.

From: *Is The Family Here To Stay?*, David Allan Hubbard, Word Books, Waco, Texas, 1971, p. 78.

—23—

Guidelines of Wisdom and Instruction

Proverbs 9:10—The fear of the Lord is the beginning of wisdom, and the knowledge of the Holy One is understanding. (NASV)

Proverbs 5:1,2—My son, give attention to my wisdom, Incline your ear to my understanding; That you may observe discretion, And your lips may reserve knowledge. (NASV)

Proverbs 4:5-7—Acquire wisdom! Acquire understanding! Do not forget, nor turn away from the words of my mouth. Do not forsake her, and she will guard you; Love her, and she will watch over you. The beginning of wisdom is: Acquire wisdom; and with all your acquiring, get understanding. (NASV)

Proverbs 2:2,7—Make your ear attentive to wisdom, Incline your heart to understanding; He stores up sound wisdom for the upright; He is a shield to those who walk in integrity. (NASV)

Proverbs 3:1-3—My son, forget not my law or teaching, but let your heart keep my commandments; For length of days, and years of a life (worth living) and tranquility (inward and outward and continuing through old age till death), these shall they add to you. Let not mercy and kindness (shutting out all hatred and selfishness), and truth (shutting out all deliberate hypocrisy or falsehood) forsake you. Bind them about your neck; write them upon the tablet of your heart. (AMP)

Looking to the Future

—24—

Growing Older

Growing older is having to make changes, is moving from endings to new beginnings. A person outlives what has gone before, and starts something new. As the writer of Ecclesiastes says, change is as certain as the seasons. It's the rhythm of saying goodby and hello at the same time, and being sad because you had to leave behind a part of yourself. Saying goodby and hello is never easy; yet it's often essential for personal growth.

From: *Friendship After Forty,* James Sparks, Abingdon Press, Nashville, Tennessee, 1980, p. 22.

The Beauty of Winter

It is the winter of my life.
   I see the snow sparkling outside
      in the twilight
Yet I am not cold or alone.
   I am warmed by the fires of my memories
And all the women of God who have lived,
   loved, and then opened their hands
      and let go
Are here with me.

Taken from: "Change Points," by Joyce Landorf, Fleming H. Revell Co., Old Tappan, New Jersey, 1981, p. 173.

—25—

Our Attitude Toward Life

Looking on life through God's lenses will arouse within you an enlarged capacity for sensitivity. Rather than just getting older, you will begin to see and think deeper, respond better, and react sooner (and much more positively) to circumstances.

Wisdom leads to understanding. Let it happen! Since the empty nest stage usually provides you with more time, take advantage of it. You can become a person of such sensitivity, others will desire your presence. But in order for that to happen, you'll need to have the same prayer on your lips as this one:

Lord, thou knowest better than I know that I am growing older, will some day be old.

Keep me from getting talkative, and particularly from the fatal habit of thinking I must say something on every subject and every occasion. Release me from craving to try to straighten out everybody's affairs. Make me thoughtful, but not moody. Helpful, but not bossy. With my vast store of wisdom it seems a pity not to use it all, but thou knowest, Lord, that I want a few friends at the end of my life.

Keep my mind free from the recital of endless details, give me wings to get to the point.

Seal my lips on my aches and pains. They are increasing and my love of rehearsing them is becoming sweeter as the years go by.

I ask for grace enough to listen to the tales of others' pains. Help me endure them patiently.

Teach me the glorious lesson that occasionally it is possible that I may be mistaken.

Keep me reasonably sweet; I do not want to be a saint: some are hard to live with, but a sour old person is one of the crowning works of the devil.

Help me to exact all possible fun out of life. There are so many funny things around us and I don't want to miss any of them.

—Anonymous

You see, understanding includes accepting and admitting our own tendencies yet trusting God to make us bigger, better people.

From: *Strike The Original Match*, Charles R. Swindoll, Multnomah Press, Portland, Oregon, 1980, pp. 188, 189.

Steady my hurried pace with a vision of the eternal reach of time.

Give me, amid the confusion of the day, the calmness of the everlasting hills.

Break the tensions of my nerves and muscles with the soothing music of the singing streams that live in my memory.

Teach me the art of taking minute vacations—of slowing down to look at a flower, to chat with a friend, to pat a dog, to smile at a child, to read a few lines from a good book.

Slow me down, Lord, and inspire me to send my roots deep into the soil of life's enduring values, that I may grow toward my greater destiny.

Remind me each day that the race is not always to the swift; that there is more to life than increasing its speed.

Let me look upward to the towering oak and know that it grew great and strong because it grew slowly and well.

—Orin L. Crain

From: *Strike The Original Match,* Charles R. Swindoll, Multnomah Press, Portland, Oregon, 1980, p. 92.

It is very important that we never conclude that only the pleasant and the beautiful have positive value. The truth of the matter is that life is a bitter-sweet reality, and that is its essence and its glory. For the final outcome both the sunshine and the shadows are needed.

A belief in providence, in a God who is at work in all things for good, can lead to that perspective on the past that enables one to say: "For all that has been, thanks!" It is one thing to look back and say: "For some of what has been, thanks!" To embrace all of life in that thanksgiving is something quite different, but it is the perspective that a belief in God's goodness and wisdom provides. Understanding life as destiny, not happenstance, and acknowledging God's hand as having been in it at all, does make for gratitude and acceptance and the ability to end one's days at peace with the past.

From: *Stages, The Art of Living the Expected,* John R. Claypool, Word Books, Waco, Texas, 1977, pp. 86-87.

—26—

The Resources We Need to Move Through Life

I Peter 1:6,7—(You should) be exceedingly glad on this account, though now for a little while you may be distressed by trials and suffer temptations, To that (the genuineness) of your faith may be tested, (your faith) which is infinitely more precious than the perishable gold which is tested and purified by fire. (This proving of your faith is intended) to redound to (your) praise and glory and honor when Jesus Christ the Messiah, the Anointed One, is revealed. (AMP)

II Timothy 1:7—For God did not give us a spirit of timidity—of cowardice, of craven and cringing and fawning fear—but (He has given us a spirit) of power and of love and of calm and well-balanced mind and discipline and self-control. (AMP)

Colossians 3:17—And whatever you do—no matter what it is—in word or deed, do everything in the name of the Lord Jesus and in (dependence upon) His Person, giving praise to God the Father through Him. (AMP)

II Corinthians 9:8—And God is able to make all grace (every favor and earthly blessing) come to you in abundance, so that you may always and under all circumstances and whatever the need, be self-sufficient—possessing enough to require no aid or support and furnished in abundance for every good work and charitable donation. (AMP)

Ephesians 2:4-6—But God! So rich is He in His mercy! Because of and in order to satisfy the great and wonderful and intense love with which He loved us, even when we were dead (slain) by (our own) shortcomings and trespasses, He made us alive together in fellowship and in union with Christ. He gave us the very life of Christ Himself, the same new life with which He quickened Him. (For) it is by grace—by His favor and mercy which you did not deserve—that you are saved (delivered from judgment and made partakers of Christ's salvation). And He raised us up together with

Him and made us sit down together—giving us joint seating with Him—in the heavenly sphere (by virtue of our being) in Christ Jesus, the Messiah, the Anointed One. (AMP)

Philippians 2:13—(Not in your own strength) for it is God who is all the while effectually at work in you—energizing and creating in you the power and desire—both to will and to work for His good pleasure and satisfaction and delight. (AMP)

James 1:2-3—When all kinds of trials and temptations crowd into your lives, my brothers, don't resent them as intruders, but welcome them as friends! Realize that they come to test your faith and to produce in you the quality of endurance. (Phillips)

Philippians 4:6-9—Don't worry over anything whatever; tell God every detail of your needs in earnest and thankful prayer, and the peace of God, which transcends human understanding, will keep constant guard over your hearts and minds as they rest in Christ Jesus. Here is a last piece of advice. If you believe in goodness and if you value the approval of God, fix your minds on the things which are holy and right and pure and beautiful and good. Model your conduct on what you have learned from me, on what I have told you and shown you, and you will find that the God of peace will be with you.

Isaiah 40:28,29,31—Have you not known? Have you not heard? The everlasting God, the Lord, the Creator of the ends of the earth, does not faint or grow weary; there is no searching of His understanding. He gives power to the faint and weary, and to him who has no might He increases strength—causing it to multiply and making it abound. But those who wait for the Lord—who expect, look for and hope in Him—shall change and renew their strength and power; they shall lift their wings and mount up (close to God) as eagles (mount up to the sun); they shall run and not be weary; they shall walk and not faint or become tired. (AMP)

Isaiah 41:10—Fear not; (there is nothing to fear) for I am with you; do not look around you in terror and be dismayed, for I am your God. I will strengthen and harden you (to difficulties); yes, I will help you; yes, I will hold you up and retain you with My victorious right hand of rightness and justice. (AMP)

Isaiah 43:1-3—But now (in spite of the past judgments for Israel's sins) thus says the Lord Who created you, O Jacob, and He Who formed You, O Israel: Fear not, for I have redeemed you—ransomed you by paying a price instead of leaving you captives; I have called you by your name, you are Mine. When you pass through the waters I will be with you, and through the rivers they shall not overwhelm you; when you walk through the fire you shall not be burned or scorched; nor shall the flame kindle upon you. For I am the Lord your God, the Holy One of Israel, your Savior; I give Egypt (to the Babylonians) for your ransom, Ethiopia and Seba (a province of Ethiopia) in exchange for your release. (AMP)

Isaiah 26:3—You will guard him and keep him in perfect and constant peace whose mind (both its inclination and its character) is stayed on You, because he commits himself to You, leans on You and hopes confidently in You. (AMP)

Proverbs 3:24-26—When you lie down you shall not be afraid; yes, you shall lie down and your sleep shall be sweet. Be not afraid of sudden terror and panic, nor of the storm and ruin of the wicked when it comes (for you will be guiltless). For the Lord shall be your confidence, firm and strong, and shall keep your foot from being caught (in a trap or hidden danger). (AMP)

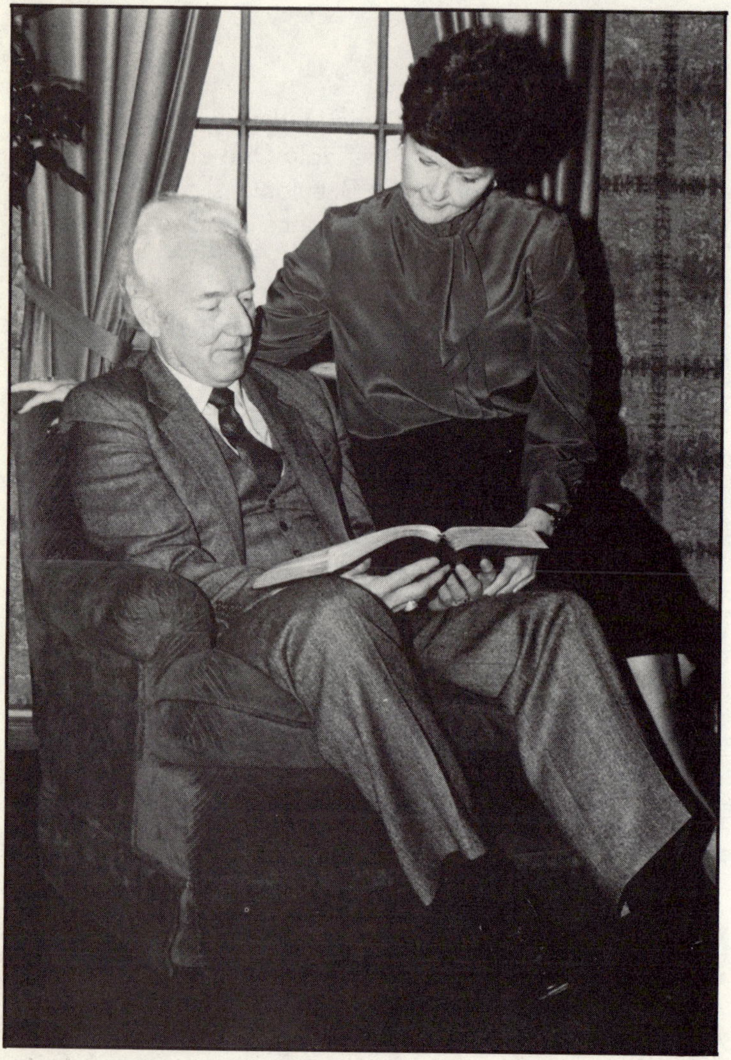

—27—

Our Exit and Entrance

From my earliest days, I had to learn to let go of some things that I had in order to get some of the things I did not have. This is what I did the day I started to school, or left home to go to work, or launched out on a new career. It turns out I have died a thousand deaths across the years, and in all of this I have learned something: every exit is also an entrance! You never leave one place without being given another. There is always new life on the other side of the door, and this is my faith as far as death is concerned. I have walked this way before. Death is an exit, to be sure, but at the same time, it is also an entrance.

I cannot think of a finer image of hope than linking "exit" and "entrance" together. The way this man came to such hope is significant as well. As he said, the last challenge of life is not so different from what we face again and again in our pilgrimage. Beginning in earliest childhood, we do have to die to smaller worlds if we are to reach bigger ones, and in every case, there is life on the other side of those crises of risk and growth. No exit ever leads us out to nowhere. Every exit is also an entrance, and learning this fact is what gives a person hope and the ability to say: "For all that will be, yes!"

From: *Stages, The Art of Living the Expected,* John R. Claypool, Word Books, Waco, Texas, 1977, pp. 88-89.

The final challenge of our earthly existence is coming to a positive and hopeful perspective about ourselves, about our past, and about our future. And how can we do this? The Gospel offers three indispensable resources: grace, providence and hope. It enables us to say three things: First, "By the grace of God, I am what I am." Secondly, "For all that has been, thanks!" And finally, "For all that will be, yes!" That statement speaks to the future. This is what a positive and hopeful existence is all about, and from the account in I

Chronicles, it appears that David achieved this goal, for we are told: "He died in a good old age, full of days, riches and honor" (29:28).

From: *Stages, The Art of Living the Expected,* John R. Claypool, Word Books, Waco, Texas, 1977, p. 89.

To the Christian, however, death is, in some ways, the pinnacle of his earthly existence, for it is at the moment of death that the Christian will know whether all that he believes is true or false. At that time, faith will be nonexistent. All of the scales of ignorance will be removed from his eyes and the mysteries of man's life will be wiped away forever.

What a joyous moment that will be, when he will be reunited with all of his loved ones who have gone on before! When, once more, the lines of communication will be reestablished, the old voices heard again, and the deathly silence at last broken forever—no more goodbyes, no more quick slipping away of loved ones into the mysterious enigma of death.

The most glorious anticipation of the Christian is, that at the time of death, he will come face-to-face with his blessed Lord, his wonderful, patient Redeemer, who all of those years continued to love him in spite of the countless times the man ignored Him and went his willful way. At death, with its immediate launching into a new life, his relationship with Christ will be different. He will see Him with the same clarity that the disciples saw Him on the road to Damascus. He will not be meeting someone new, but rather Someone with whom he has been intimate, more intimate than with any other person. For only Christ can share all of the moments of our lives. It is good for us to remember that the Lord is with us, not only at those times when we ignore Him as though He did not exist. He is not only with us at the heights of our goodness, but at the very depths of our evilness. In the words of the Psalmist, "Whither shall I go from my spirit? Or whither shall I flee from thy presence? If I ascend up into heaven, thou art there: if I make my bed in hell, behold, thou art there" (Psalm 139:7,8). Once we accept Him as our Redeemer, Christ is with us every step of the way. So we will not be encountering a stranger, but the best and the most intimate friend that we have ever had. When we think of death as a time of revelation and reunion, we immediately remove its venom. We can say with the apostle Paul, "O death, where is thy sting? O grave, where is thy victory?" (I Corinthians 15:55).

From: *Half-Way Up The Mountain,* David C. Morley, M.D., Fleming H. Revell Co., Old Tappan, New Jersey, 1979, pp. 77, 78.

—28—

Our Heavenly Family

We have a home ahead and we have something to be certain about when we tell homeless people this good news, whether they are street urchins or neglected old people. There is a Family—with a Heavenly Father to whom they may belong and where they may go—into which birth is by choice. However, if we have time left in the land of the living and any opportunity at all, we should make a resolve, God helping us, to make our human family as close as possible to what it should be.

From: *What Is a Family?* Edith Schaeffer, Fleming H. Revell Company, Old Tappan, New Jersey, 1975, p. 52.

Looking back over the years, they have been wonderful and heartbreaking, frustrating and joyous—all rolled into one. We have been two people constantly learning to blend our personalities and wills into that mystical union—marriage. . . . The prayer we pray for ourselves, we pray for you: "to be brought ever closer together each day."

—Joan Winmill Brown

From: *Into The High Country*, H. Norman Wright, Multnomah Press, Portland, Oregon, 1979, Preface.

—29—

Our Final Stage of Life

II Corinthians 5:1—For we know that if the tent which is our earthly home is destroyed (dissolved), we have from God a building, a house not made with hands, eternal in the heavens. (AMP)

II Corinthians 4:7-10—However, we possess this precious treasure (the divine Light of the Gospel) in (frail, human) vessels of earth, that the grandeur and exceeding greatness of the power may be shown to be of God, and not from ourselves.

We are hedged in (pressed) on every side—troubled and oppressed in every way; but not cramped or crushed; we suffer embarrassments and are perplexed and unable to find a way out, but not driven to despair;

We are (persecuted and hard driven), pursued, but not deserted—to stand alone; we are struck down to the ground, but never struck out and destroyed;

Always carrying about in the body the liability and exposure to the same putting to death that the Lord Jesus suffered, so that the (resurrection) life of Jesus also may be shown forth by and in our bodies. (AMP)

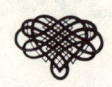